Learn Fol... ...th the M...
John Denver

Recording Credits:
Pat Bianculli: guitar
John Kilgore: recording engineer

Cherry Lane Music Company
Educational Director/Project Supervisor: Susan Poliniak
Director of Publications: Mark Phillips

ISBN 1-57560-779-4

Visit our website at www.cherrylane.com

Table of Contents

John Denver—His Music, His Life

In 1976, singer-songwriter John Denver co-founded a not-for-profit environmental education organization called the Windstar Foundation. The foundation takes a holistic approach to the myriad of problems that face our environment today. He often stated that we should stop trying to find a scapegoat for these issues. According to Denver and his group, both the problems and the solutions begin within us. In a sense, we all leave footprints on our home planet.

It may seem peculiar to begin a music instruction book by calling up just one of John Denver's many accomplishments—and a non-musical one at that—but within these thoughts about life on this planet, and how we all need to work together to find solutions to the problems we ourselves have created, lie the inspiration, the rhyme, and the reason for both the music and the life of John Denver.

Denver's music, like a footprint in the forest or a fossil in stone, remains with us years after the songs were composed. His melodies, clear and uncomplicated, seem to have been written that way on purpose—so that as many people could sing and remember them as possible. He was all about accessibility.

John Denver loved to fly, and his love for flying inspired much of the music he wrote. It was his way of getting as close to nature as he could—touching the infinite in a way most of us only dream we can.

In 1986, John Denver was one of the candidates selected to become the "first civilian in space," scheduled to fly in the space shuttle *Challenger*, but the teacher Sharon Christa McAuliffe was chosen instead. He had dreamed of writing a song in space and instead wrote "Flying for Me" as a tribute to McAuliffe and her crewmates who perished on the mission.

Flying for Me

Words and Music by
John Denver

Well, I guess that you probably know by now
I was one who wanted to fly.
I wanted to ride on that arrow of fire right up into heaven.
And I wanted to go for every man,
Every child, every mother of children.
I wanted to carry the dreams of all people right up to the stars.

And I prayed that I'd find that answer there,
Or maybe I would find the song
Giving a voice to all of the hearts that cannot be heard.
And for all of the ones who live in fear
And all of those who stand apart,
My being there would bring us a little step closer together.

They were flying for me,
They were flying for everyone.
They were trying to see a brighter day for each and everyone.
They gave us their light,

They gave us their spirit and all they could be.
They were flying for me,
They were flying for me.

And I wanted to wish on the Milky Way
And dance upon a falling star.
I wanted to give myself and free myself, enjoin myself with it all!
Given the chance to dream, it can be done,
The promise of tomorrow is real.
Children of spaceship Earth, the future belongs to us all.

It is fitting that John expressed himself through folk music. It is a timeless style, but one that changes with the times—it is simultaneously traditional and contemporary. His guitar playing decorated his simple melodies and made the songs sound fresh, even by today's standards. Learning how to play his music affords the student a trip through the history of folk guitar. These songs have much to teach us about the techniques of guitar playing: strumming, fingerpicking, moving bass notes, hammer-ons, etc. More importantly, Denver's guitar playing can teach us how to use our talents in the best way possible in order to communicate the message each song has to offer.

For John Denver, music was indeed a universal language. He believed that music allowed people in all parts of the globe to speak with the same heart and spirit. Despite differences in culture, politics, faith, or economics, we are all the same. This, for me, approaches the real definition of folk music.

More than anything else, this book is meant to be a journey down a familiar country road, up a less-traveled mountain path, and into the clouds. While learning the skills necessary for good folk guitar playing, you can also learn much about the person of John Denver. May his music become, as it was for me, an inspiration to learn more about this man and his incredible musical legacy.

TRACK 01

Note: Track 1 contains tuning pitches.

About the Author

Pasquale Bianculli

Born and raised in Brooklyn, NY, Pasquale Bianculli began playing the guitar at the age of 13 under Joseph Cassano. In 1972, he began intensive study in classical guitar with Jerry Willard and Edgard Dana at the Guitar Workshop in Oyster Bay, NY. He received his M. Mus. degree from the State University of New York at Stony Brook in 1981, and holds a certificate from Teachers College Columbia University as a Performing Artist in the Schools. As a recitalist, he has been heard across the U.S., Canada, Europe, and the Caribbean. In 1983, he made his New York solo debut at Weill Recital Hall at Carnegie Hall. He has had the honor of performing for the legendary guitarist Andres Segovia in Granada, Spain. Both he and his wife, flutist Kathy McDonald, taught at the Edna Manley School of the Arts in Kingston, Jamaica, performing throughout that country. Together with guitarist Harris Becker, he formed Guitar x2 and, in 1999, released a CD of music for two guitars, *Catgut Flambo*, on the Musicians Showcase Recordings label. The composer Carlo Domeniconi wrote and dedicated his *Long Island Suite* to the duo in 2002. Pat has been on the faculties of Dowling College and the Rocky Ridge Music Center in Colorado and has served as adjudicator in music competitions sponsored by Queens College and the American String Teacher's Association. Currently, he is on the faculty of C. W. Post Campus of Long Island University and the United Nations International School. This is his second book for Cherry Lane Music Publishing, his first being *101 Tips and Tricks for Acoustic Guitar*.

Acknowledgments

This book is dedicated to Kathleen.

Thanks to Susan Poliniak for her help throughout this project, to Kathleen McDonald for her assistance and continued support, and to Joe Turzo for the use of his photographs here.

The Basics

I know you are anxious to get to the nitty gritty of this book: the strums, the fingerpicking patterns, and some really great songs. But before you dig in, browse carefully through this chapter. You will find some helpful suggestions on how best to use the materials presented here. This chapter will also introduce you to the first of the *Technique Tips* that appear throughout the book and can help you with various technique issues.

■ Your Tools for This Journey

Guitar

John Denver played his songs on a six-string, jumbo acoustic, steel-string guitar. He also used a 12-string guitar in many of his songs. For our purposes, a good six-string, steel-string acoustic that is adjusted properly for easy playing or a nylon-string guitar will do. Bear in mind that it's easier to fingerpick and to fret chords with a nylon-string guitar. It is the guitar I recommend especially to beginner and intermediate students, but if your steel-string is adjusted properly, it should do just fine.

Capo

Most of Denver's songs are in "easy guitar keys" such as G and D. Since we don't all have voices with the same range as John's, transposing via the use of a capo can make the songs easier to sing. Also, the capo can help if you want to play along with Denver's recordings (not *all* of which are in G and D!), which I recommend to all diligent students. Capos come in various styles. Choose one with its metal parts covered by rubber or some other non-abrasive material, assuring that there is virtually no contact with the wood of the guitar.

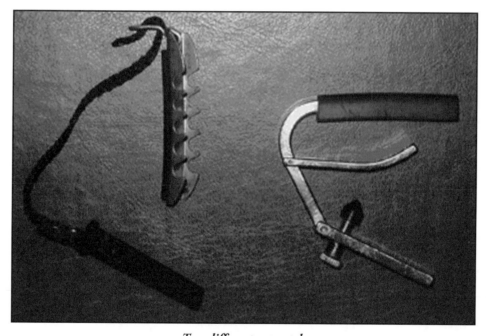

Two different capo styles

Flatpick and Fingers

This book teaches both flatpick and fingerpicking styles. Denver himself used a *thumb pick* (a flatpick that wraps around the thumb) and fingers.

Musical Skills

The ability to read standard and tab staves, as well as the basic chords in first position, is assumed. You can get this information from any good beginner's guitar method. Where practical, I have included review material here.

Aural Skills

Make sure your ear becomes familiar with Denver's music. Listen to his songs and pay attention to the sounds of the guitar parts. It seems like an obvious point to make, but many guitar students don't give their aural skills enough exercise.

One Man—So Many Songs

Many of us have grown up listening only to the greatest hits of John Denver, of which there have been many. I continue to be impressed by the depth of emotion expressed in some of the lesser-known songs in his collection. Many of them reveal Denver's contemplative side, which doesn't always come across in his big hits. This book culls material from both of these groups. In some cases, I have used only a portion of a song as an example, while others are included in full versions.

■ Practice Advice

Don't forget to take breaks in between exercises during your practice sessions. Breaks allow your muscles to stop flexing and extending for a bit. When you practice for 15–20 minutes straight, take the next five off.

At any point in this book where a problem arises, take the time to analyze what the problem might be: right hand, left hand, coordination of both hands, etc. In most cases, slow, methodical, and relaxed practicing should get you easily through each musical example.

■ About the Music Examples

The music, both the short technical exercises as well as the longer arrangements, are to be practiced with both tab and notes. The tab tells what the notes don't and vice versa. What exactly do I mean? Even if you can read standard notation well, it is the tab that will tell you exactly where to play a particular passage of music in terms of frets and strings. This is very important for getting the exact sound that a passage requires. On the other hand, music notation tells you the exact rhythms to play and how long to hold one note while a new note sounds, neither of which are included in tab notation.

■ A Review of the Fundamentals

Every teacher has his or her own "to-do" list for when a new student comes in for a first lesson. Here are three key items that are on most teachers' lists. Every well-meaning guitarist should master all of them. They are key for the proper playing of folk music, or indeed any sort of music on an acoustic guitar. You probably learned them when you first picked up a guitar, but let's review before we begin the nuts-and-bolts work of folk guitar.

Playing Position

How a person sits and holds a guitar says much about the way he or she will sound on the instrument. Is the position open and comfortable, or tight and scrunched? Teachers and students often search together for the most natural playing position, which is the one that allows the guitar to become an extension of the player's body. We are talking, of course, about *sitting* with the guitar. You can stand if you wish, but after a while you will really have sore feet!

No matter how you hold your guitar, you must make sure that you are sitting comfortably in your chair. Sit in a straight-backed chair, preferably at the edge of the seat. Drop both arms to your side. Keep a slight arch in the lower back, as this helps prevent fatigue. After the muscles are built up properly, you will be able to play for a much longer amount of time. Now, hold your guitar the way you normally would to play.

In trying to establish a good playing position, you should take note of how your body moves most naturally. For instance, if you were to bring your elbow out and away from your body while holding the guitar as in the photo below . . .

. . . it would only be a short while before your left arm became too tired to play. Instead, you should try to move your joints, elbows, shoulders, and wrists in the most natural way possible. In the photo below, the shoulder is relaxed and the elbow remains close to the body.

Now, look further down the arm to the wrist. The wrist should never bend while playing. Rather, the left arm should keep a straight line from the elbow to almost the first joint of the fingers. This is *very important!*

Finally, the neck of your guitar should sit close to the palm with your left-hand thumb parallel to the frets of the instrument behind the neck.

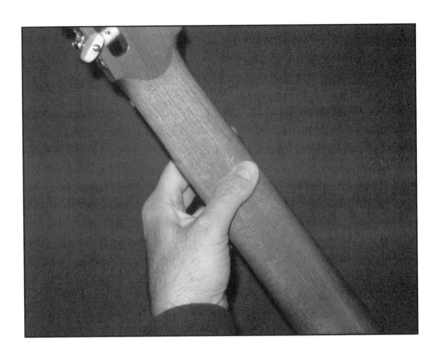

Scales

Scales show off any student's ability (or lack thereof) to coordinate the hands in a rhythmic and musical way. Are the notes connected or detached? Is the left hand moving faster than the right? These are good questions to keep in mind.

TRACK 02

Try playing the above C major scale in first position. You can use a pick or your fingers. When you can play this scale smoothly (no pauses and with a steady tempo) and you don't have to think about where the next note is, the next objective is to listen to what you are playing. You should hear no gaps between the notes, no places where you cannot hear a vibration from the string; one note should morph seamlessly into the next. This is not so easy to do at first, but with practice it can bring you to another level of awareness about your playing. Your scales become more *musical.*

If you are using a pick, you can pick all of the notes as *downstrokes* (catching the string[s] with a downward movement). When you want to play faster, you should use *alternate picking*—alternate *upstrokes* (catching the string[s] with an upward movement) and downstrokes and avoid playing consecutive "downs" or "ups."

Chord Changes

Accurate and speedy chord switching is the next technique teachers look for. As with the scales, listen for chords that are out of time, muffled, or out of sync with the strumming or picking hand. Just to warm up, try a simple chord-switching exercise. Play the first position G and D chords to a metronome click of 60 *BPM* (beats per minute). Start out with one chord change every four beats. When you're comfortable with that, try one every three beats, then one every two, and eventually one every beat. When you feel confident with that, raise the bar even further by speeding up the metronome. See how fast you can go!

■ Basic Right-Hand Technique

Let's review some specific right-hand skills.

Playing with a Pick

There are many ways to hold a pick. I offer you one that takes advantage of the larger arm muscles rather than the more fragile muscles of the fingers. By training your arm to absorb most of the repetitive energy of playing, your right hand can remain more relaxed and "natural." You can avoid injury, have a much bigger sound, and not tire as quickly. A picture is worth a thousand guitar picks (and is a lot cheaper!), so here goes. Notice the placement of the fingers and the grip.

The right arm should rest comfortably on the edge of the guitar by the bridge. Your right hand should be relaxed and the fingers naturally curled into your palm. The thumb should extend forward of the fingers. Hold the pick firmly but comfortably between the thumb and index finger as shown in the photo. When you play, the motion of the arm from your elbow should move the pick—not the tip joints of the thumb and index fingers. Those tiny muscles should be used only to *hold* the pick.

Now, move your right arm down and up while you play the 1st string. Start by hitting that one string only, then add in the 2nd string, then the 3rd, and so on. If you are having trouble accurately hitting one string, try playing the exercise backwards—start by hitting all six strings and work backwards towards just the 1st. Always play your exercises slowly at first until the muscles involved feel warmed up.

TRACK 03

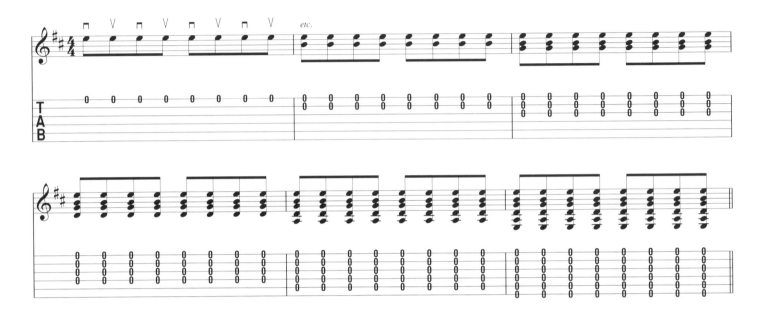

Fingerpicking

For the music in this book, the fingers of the right hand are indicated by the letter names found in most classical guitar methods. The thumb is indicated by *p* (for *pulgar*), the index finger by *i*, the middle finger by *m*, and the ring finger by *a* (for *anular*).

On the right is a photo of good right-hand positioning for fingerpicking.

Notice that the right hand is relaxed and the thumb is in front of the fingers. The wrist is straight, allowing tendons, nerves, and blood to move freely through the carpal tunnel. You should never plant a right-hand finger on the face of the guitar; this both impedes the movement of the hand and muffles some of the overtones.

To ease you into the world of fingerpicking, try this right-hand exercise: a simple arpeggio.

Place your right-hand fingers on the strings in a fashion similar to the photo: thumb (p) on the 4th string, index finger (i) on the 3rd, middle finger (m) on the 2nd, and ring finger (a) on the 1st. Play one finger at a time in the pattern p–i–m–a. As you play, flex each finger inwards towards the palm of the hand, using as much of the nail or fingertip as you can to make contact with the string. This should give you a good idea of what fingerpicking feels like on the guitar. Once you feel comfortable with this, move your hand to the 5th–4th–3rd–2nd string combination, and then to the 6th–5th–4th–3rd combination.

■ Basic Left-Hand Technique

A great deal of John Denver's music (although not all!) is played with basic chords in open position. This is a good time to review some basic progressions and to get the feel of these chords into your fingers. Try these on for size, using a basic one-quarter-note-per-strum feel—or, if you're feeling adventurous, try the 4–3–2–1 string combination for fingerpicking, one note/string for each quarter note beat.

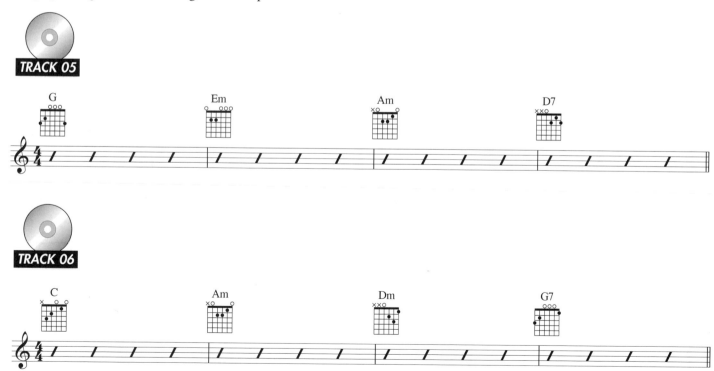

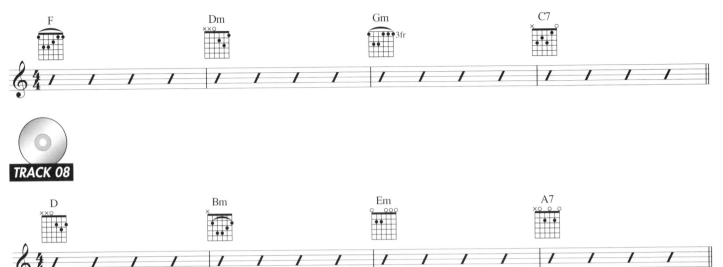

F   Dm   Gm   C7

D   Bm   Em   A7

Technique Tip #1
Help with Barre Chords

While living abroad in the Caribbean, a friend took me for my first visit to a supermarket. Everything looked different—the vegetables were smaller than what we were used to, but the fruit was much larger. My friend gave me a good piece of advice: "Buy only what you need, not what you see." His very astute and helpful comment can be adapted to barre chords: Barre only the notes you need, not all of the notes you see.

Most people press their barring finger (here, the 1st finger) down on too many strings. But there is a better way to play barre chords, one where you won't tire so easily or wind up with sore muscles: Press down *only* on the notes needed in the barre. For the F chord, for example, you fret with other fingers on the 3rd, 4th, and 5th strings, so it's not important that you barre *behind* all of that—it's wasted effort. So, with your barring finger, apply pressure on only the 6th, 2nd, and 1st strings by curving your finger. Your 1st finger should look more concave than flat, with the *proximal joint* (the joint closest to the palm) making contact with strings 1 and 2, as in the photo. This is much easier to manage and gets the job done.

F

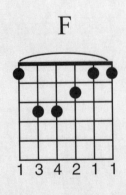

1 3 4 2 1 1

Strumming Techniques

The simplest way to begin a foray into folk guitar is with strumming. By the end of this chapter, you should be able to play some pretty impressive right-hand strum patterns that you'll find useful for many types of songs. Each new strum pattern here builds on the previous one. Although these strums are presented as accompaniments to various John Denver songs, they are adaptable to other songs and styles that use the acoustic guitar. These include alternative folk, world music, blues, and country.

In this chapter, although the instruction is mainly for strumming with fingers, you can generally use either a flatpick or fingers to strum. If you decide to go with a pick, take a look at the *Playing with a Pick* section of the previous chapter if you haven't already. And remember, the pick should be moved by the motion of the *arm*, not the *fingers*.

■ Strumming with the Fingers

Although any of the fingers can be used, in this section you should primarily strum with the middle *(m)* finger of the right hand to keep your thumb *(p)* free to play bass notes and your other fingers ready to embellish the strum pattern later on.

With your thumb held parallel to the strings and resting on the 6th string, quickly flick your fingers outward in such a way that the middle finger strikes across the top three or four strings. It's not important exactly how many strings you play right now—just get a feel for strumming first. The motion of extending the fingers to flick the strings should be quick. Relax the hand back into the initial position after each strum.

■ Simple Strum Accompaniments

The strum patterns in this section are used in many of John Denver's songs. Most of his songs are in 4/4 (also known as *common time*) or 2/2 (also known as *cut time*), which is usually just a fast 4/4 (in fact, you'll notice on the CD that the "clicks" to set the tempo for the examples in 2/2 are two measures of four quarter notes). The strumming patterns can be adapted for songs in 3/4 time, however.

Take Me Home, Country Roads

Words and Music by
John Denver, Bill Danoff and Taffy Nivert

Let's start with an example from a famous John Denver song for which you'll use just four chords: G, Em, D, and C. When you can play this well, you'll feel as though your boots are kickin' up the dust on some back road in the mountains of West Virginia.

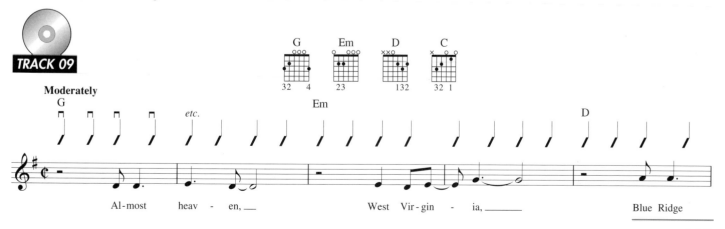

Don't try to both strum and sing if you're doing this sort of thing for the first time. To start with, what you want to be able to do here is strum once on each quarter note beat. Play each note as a downstroke (indicated by the bracket-like symbol above the staff). Make sure the chord changes are nice and clean. If strumming each beat is too difficult for now, either slow down your playing or play only every other quarter note beat—in other words, play on just the first and third beats of each measure. You can also strum just the first beat of each measure if this concept is really new to you and you want to set a firm foundation for your technique. When you feel confident with that, challenge yourself with the "every other beat" approach, and then work yourself up to playing on each quarter note beat. Play along to a metronome set to 60 just to start with each of these approaches, and increase the tempo when you can.

16

When you feel comfortable with strumming once for each quarter note beat, try adding in the lyrics. If this is too much to think about at one time, try reciting just the lyrics in rhythm to a metronome beat a few times. When you can manage this, try singing or reciting and playing together. Practice until you feel comfortable strumming and singing at the same time before moving on.

◼ A Little Technique Check

Before moving on to the next section, you should be able to:

- Strum a steady beat.
- Change chords smoothly without stopping the music.
- Sing or recite lyrics while strumming.

◼ A Simple Bass–Strum Accompaniment

In this accompaniment pattern, you play a bass note with your thumb (on the 4th, 5th, or 6th string) followed by a strum with the middle finger on the treble strings. Instead of the simple strum pattern where you downstrummed once per beat, here you're going to alternate each strum with a bass note like this: *bass–strum–bass–strum*. You should hear not only the chords, but also a separate bass part played by your thumb. This fills out the accompaniment nicely.

The following exercise, using just open strings, prepares you to play the bass–strum pattern as well as the other alternating bass patterns taught in this chapter. Practice this slowly and rhythmically at first. After a few tries, your thumb should be able to accurately strike the correct bass strings.

If you're fingerpicking, the thumb plays (downstroke) on beats 1 and 3, and after each bass note you should strum the open strings with your middle finger as you did in the basic strum exercise. For you flatpickers out there, pick the bass note and perform the strum with the pick—no fingers. Take a look at Technique Tip #2 in this chapter to get a feel for the principles of movement.

TRACK 10

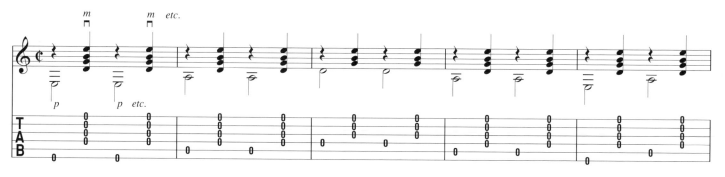

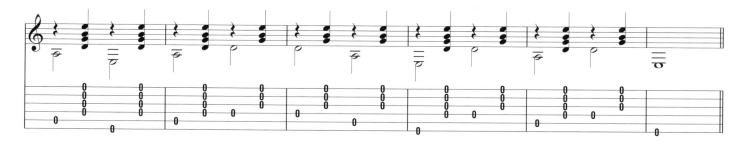

Technique Tip #2
Feel the Weight

A good thumb stroke comes not from the tip joint of the thumb and the small muscles in the fingers, but rather from the larger muscles found in the arm, shoulder, and even the upper back. It is the weight of the arm that gives good volume and tone to a stroke. Using the thumb in this way also gives a good "bounce" to the rhythm and helps prevent injury due to repetitive strain on the hand. Try the following exercise.

With the left side of the thumbnail placed on the 4th string, try to "feel the weight" of your entire arm and hand. As your thumb continues holding on to the string, you should start to feel the tension of the string up into your arm and shoulder. Engaging the larger muscles of your arm and back is the hallmark of good technique and tone production on the guitar. Now, let your arm drop to the floor, allowing the thumb to play the 4th string. *Bohnng!!* Did you hear that? It sounded like Big Ben! That's the sound of a great thumb stroke. Repeat this exercise until it feels natural to you.

This is a good technique builder, and, with practice, it can improve the volume and tone of your thumb stroke. But while playing in a real-world situation, you really don't have enough time to drop your arm to the floor each time you use your thumb! You need to keep your right hand close to the strings while playing, but you can still use this technique. Concentrate on engaging at least the larger joint of the thumb (where it connects to the palm), and release the thumb from the string so that it moves only as far as the adjacent string, with that larger joint doing most of the movement. This way, your hand never moves too far from the correct playing position.

Let's return to "Country Roads" so you can apply what you've learned about the bass–strum accompaniment. Now that you will be changing chords with this technique, note that the bass notes should be determined by the chords. You'll generally use the bottom one or two notes of a chord; you'll eventually get a feel for what sounds best. For now, use the 6th-string note for the G chord, the 6th-string note for Em, the 4th-string note for the D chord, and the 5th-string note for the C.

Written out, it looks like this. Play through it a few times until you feel comfortable. Go as slowly as you need to when you first approach this. You'll want to get this technique down, as it's an important building block. Make sure you can sing *and* play this at the same time before you move on.

TRACK 11

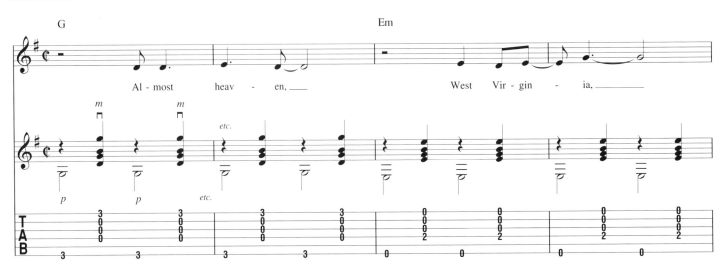

■ Alternating Basses

"Country Roads" is going to take a few interesting turns now. In this next setting, you'll play the chords and sing the melody the same as before, but now the bass will have more to do. It will almost sound as though a second melody has been added to the bottom part of the song. Alternating bass notes—using two or more bass notes per chord—can lend a feeling of movement to an arrangement. It also helps strengthen your technique as you learn to move the thumb accurately from string to string.

Chord	Bass Note: First Choice	Bass Note: Second Choice	Bass Note: Third Choice
G	6th string	4th string	5th string
Em	6th string	5th string	4th string
D	4th string	5th string	3rd string
C	5th string	4th string	6th string

For this version, I used the chord tones from the above chart and chose which to play based on my own musical tastes. One good rule to follow is that if the melody of a song is very jagged with big interval leaps, it's best to choose a more stable and slow-changing bass part to balance out the melodic movement. On the other hand, if the melody moves smoothly, as it does in "Country Roads," you are free to use pretty much whatever kind of bass you'd like.

TRACK 12

West Vir - gin - ia, _____ moun - tain mom - ma, _____

take _ me home, _____ coun - try roads. _____

Technique Tip #3
Plant the Thumb

While you are strumming, practice planting your thumb on the next bass note to be played. This technique both anchors the right hand firmly on the guitar and prepares the next bass note accurately. Remember to never move the thumb from the little or "tip" joint—use instead the larger joint close to the palm to play.

■ The Basic Bass–Flick/Back Strum

The *flick/back* technique is another piece of equipment in the essential strumming arsenal. Along with the melody note (played with the middle finger), you hear a *plink-plinka* rhythm that is the characteristic sound of a style of banjo playing called *ol' timey*. The technique itself is called *frailing*. On the banjo, it is played using the middle finger to strum down on the strings; on the way down, the thumb grabs and plucks the banjo's high 5th string. When the flick/back strum is played properly on the guitar, the sound produced is similar to frailing and works well for songs with moderate to quick tempos.

In 2/2, flick/backs generally occur on the second halves of beats 1 and 2, and in 4/4 they appear on beats 2 and 4. Rest the thumb on the 6th string as in the previous exercise. Open the fist as you would to play the simple strum, striking the treble strings with a middle-finger downstroke, but instead of immediately relaxing the hand, let the index finger sweep back *up* across the strings, sounding at least the first two or three strings.

It's not important how many strings you play on the upstroke. You can also do this strum with the middle finger playing both the downstroke and upstroke, but it is better technique to play with both the middle and the index fingers. Practice this treble-strings-only exercise until it feels and sounds relaxed and you're ready to add in the bass notes.

Now you can apply this pattern to "Country Roads," focusing on the Chorus of the song. If it is too difficult to use the alternating bass style, you can go back to playing one bass note per chord until you become more comfortable with this new technique.

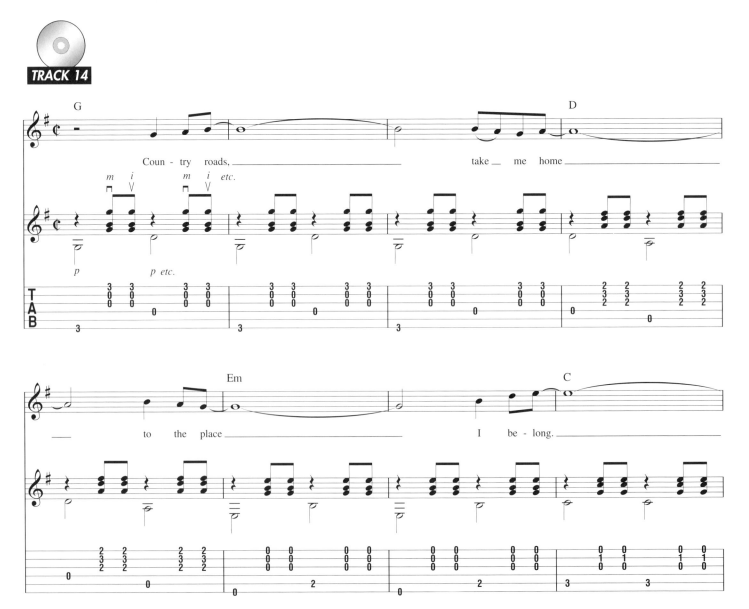

Flick/Back Variation #1—Playing in 3/4 Time

The flick/back pattern is versatile and can be used to accompany songs in 3/4 time; just a slight modification from the previous pattern is necessary. Hold down a G chord and play the following.

TRACK 15

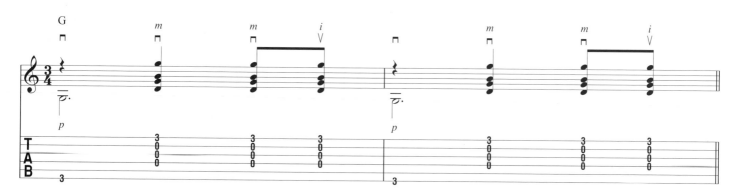

The accent falls on the first beat, which is always a bass note. The second beat is a single downstrum with the middle finger (flick) on the treble strings, and the third beat is where you add the flick/back, also on the treble strings, with the middle and index fingers, respectively.

Starwood in Aspen

Try the 3/4 version of the flick/back as the accompaniment to this beautiful John Denver song, a waltz written about his home in Colorado. Watch out for the fourth measure from the end—there's a chord change in the middle of the measure.

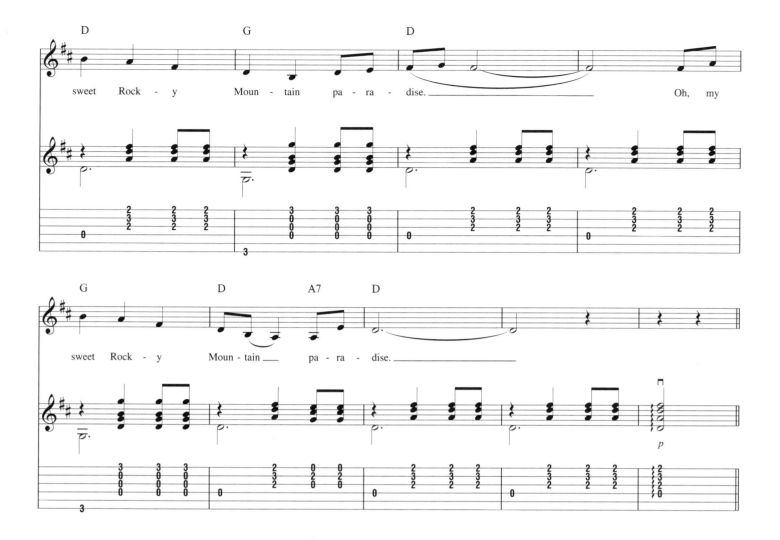

Flick/Back Variation #2—The Swing Feel, or a "Flexible" Beat

If you played the flick/back strum exactly as written (bass–flick–flick/back) it should sound pretty good—but you can make it sound even better.

Rhythm in most styles of music can be very flexible, even elastic. Don't get me wrong—downbeats should always be rhythmically precise. But the space between the downbeats can often be thought of as a little more "free." This is one of the reasons why orchestras have conductors. Left to their own devices, each instrumentalist would play their notes *slightly different* than the other musicians. The conductor's job is to keep the members together so that their *slightly different* interpretations of the rhythm don't stray too far from the score. Good musicians are able to "play" with rhythm without losing their sense of the beat. One of the ways in which to "play" like this is to swing eighth notes ever so slightly.

If you've never worked with a swing feel before, you'll want to start off slowly—set your metronome for 60 BPM. The first and second beats in the following exercise are the same as in the previous flick/back examples. In that third beat, however, flick down on the first note of the triplet and then back on the third note. If you learned triplets by verbalizing them, you flick down on the "tri," do nothing on "pl," and go back up on the "let."

Hold down a G chord and try this new feel on for size.

TRACK 17

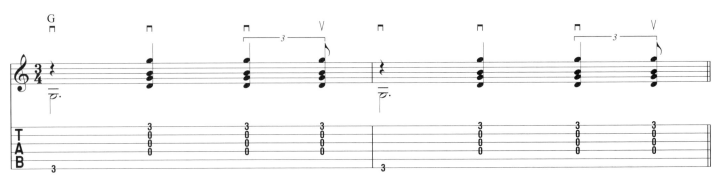

As you repeat the pattern, you may notice that it removes any stiffness from the rhythmic feel, making it more pliable, more "jazzy."

Here is a section of "Starwood in Aspen" written out with swing eighths in the flick/back. When you get a feel for this, try going back to the full song and playing it all the way through with this in mind.

TRACK 18

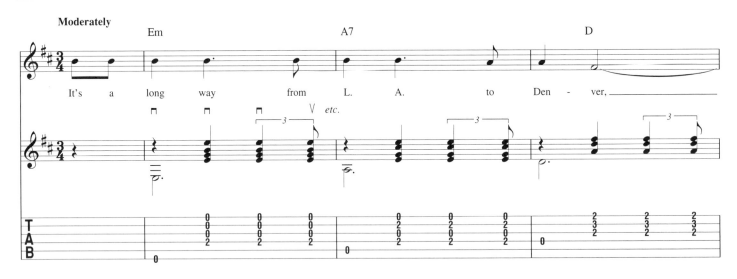

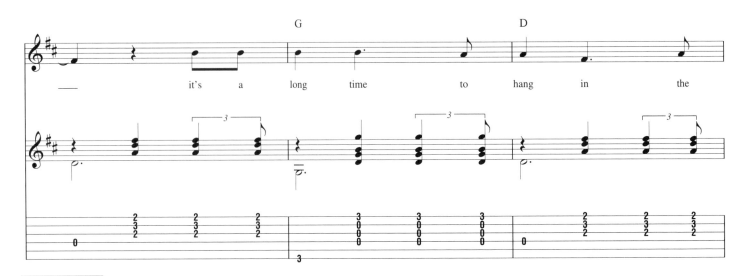

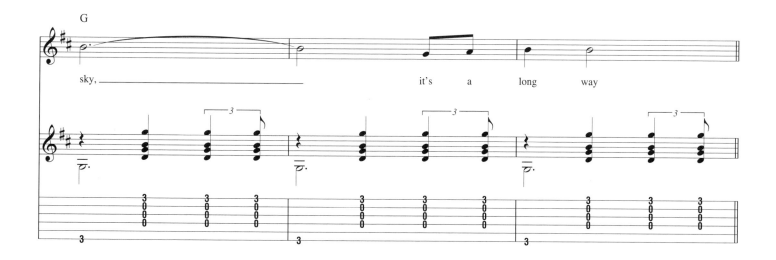

Flick/Back Variation #3—Filling in the Gaps

This next variation is a very useful one. I have heard it played both slowly and quickly in many of John Denver's songs. It creates a seamless strum pattern that keeps the rhythm chugging along. The pattern, *p-i*-flick/back, is a sort of hybrid strum/fingerpicking pattern in that it uses not only the thumb to pick a separate string but also the index finger. I placed it here with the strumming patterns because it's more closely related to the flick/back strum than any of the fingerpicking patterns to come.

Here's a primer exercise. Rest your thumb on any of the bass strings and your index finger on the 3rd string (don't worry about your left hand right now). Play a bass note *downwards* with your thumb and then pluck the 3rd string *upwards* with your index finger.

I know—this is all well and good, but where does the index finger figure into the strum pattern? I'm glad you asked that question. The index finger playing the 3rd string comes before the flick/back part of the strum, filling in that eighth note "gap" in the pattern. Try the following on for size.

TRACK 19

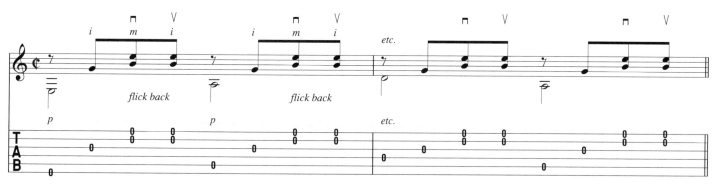

Two Different Directions

Words and Music by
John Denver

Here's a great little excerpt from a Denver tune that works well with this new pattern.

■ Flick/Back Variation #4—Neighbor Note Hammer-Ons in the Bass

Chord tones are the actual notes in a chord, and *neighbor notes* in this context "live" directly next to them on the staff and may not be a part of the chord at all. For instance, a C would be a neighbor note to B or D in a G chord. Neighbor notes are great devices for ornamenting a bass line in a fingerpicking pattern. Take a look at the following example.

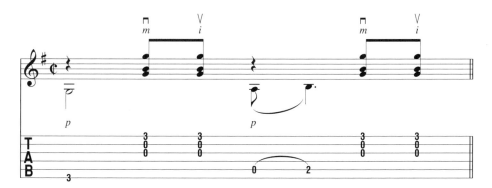

On the 5th string, play the note B on the 5th string—a chord tone. Its lower neighbor is an open A. You can hammer-on from that non–chord tone A up to the chord tone B. The way that you play it is like this: You essentially play the bass-flick/back as you've learned it, but on the third beat of the measure, "unfret" your left-hand 2nd finger and strike the open A on the 5th string as if it was a regular bass note and then hammer on the B. This is then followed with the usual flick/back. Nice, eh?

Technically, any note in a chord can fall victim to a "drive-by hammer-on." Some will sound better than others, and the choice is up to the player. For a D chord, hammering on from the open 3rd-string G to the 2nd-fret A sounds good, and in a C chord, hammering on from the open 4th-string D to the 2nd-fret E sounds nice, too. Also, the rhythm, although written as straight eighth notes, can be swung instead.

Technique Tip #4
Nailing Those Hammer-Ons and Pull-Offs

Here's a short refresher course. Pluck the open D string with the right-hand thumb or flatpick, as per your preferred method. While the note is ringing, hammer down on the second fret of that D string (the E) with the 2nd finger of your left hand. The motion should be quick and relaxed yet deliberate. To get the best sound, keep the fretting finger naturally curved and hammer on just behind the 2nd fret. It is actually the string touching the fret that changes the pitch.

After pull-off

A pull-off is simply the reverse of a hammer-on. Once again, the left hand is used to make the sound—this time by actually plucking the string somewhat. This time, fret and play the D-string E note (2nd fret) as above and pull off to the open D. Don't try to lift up the left-hand finger from the string, as this will never produce a sound loud enough to be heard above all of the other sounds coming from your guitar. Instead, pluck across the 4th string with the finger in the direction of the 3rd string. The finger should land on the 3rd string as pictured.

The following exercise can be used to build strength and coordination for playing both hammer-ons and pull-offs. Start on the 4th string and play the following pattern.

TRACK 22

Repeat on all of the strings using different fingering/fretting combinations: 1–2, 1–3, 1–4, 2–3, 2–4, 3–4. After you feel confident with hammering on with this pattern, "reverse" it and play the intervals as pull-offs.

TRACK 23

With all of this hammering, you might have thought I was training you to become a carpenter! So let's take another walk down "Country Roads" before you start asking me what a screwdriver is.

For practical purposes right now, you will hammer on only once per measure in "Country Roads," and this will occur on the third beat. Here is the Chorus to "Country Roads" one last time. The accompaniment is infused with alternating basses, hammer-ons, and flick/backs. How far this is from our original accompaniment!

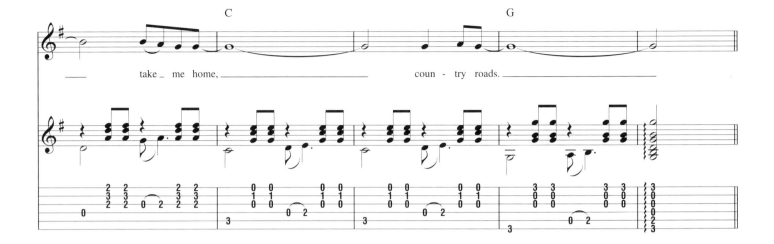

Bass Runs

Bass runs are fragments of scales that are used to bridge two chords together. They can provide smoother transitions between chords than just the same old strum patterns. Take a look at the following example.

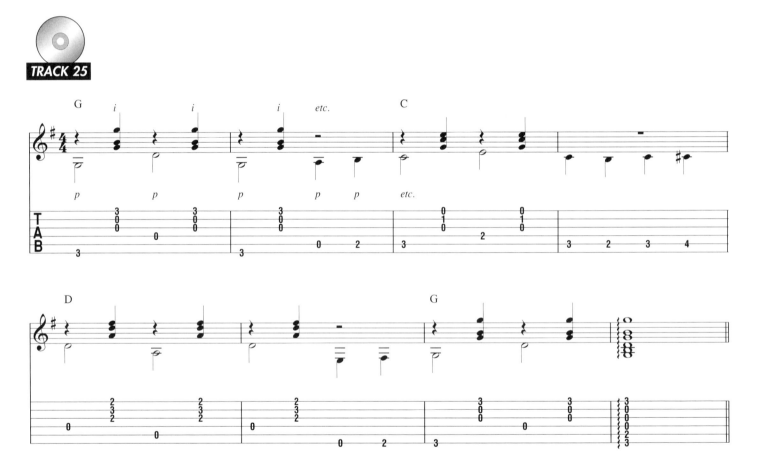

Notice in measure 2 that the strum pattern has been stopped and a two-note bass run has been added (A to B). This provides a step-wise passage to the bass of the C chord. There's another run in measure 4, where the steps are only a half step apart (*chromatic*) on their way from the C chord to the D, but they achieve the same smoothness as in the previous run. For the switch from D back to G in measure 6, the bass goes down the octave so you won't run out of notes to play—merely a choice based on practicality, although the end sounds great leading to that big, fat, low G on the 6th string.

■ Playing the Melody in the Bass—Carter Family Style

Bass runs can allow you to add some melody to an accompaniment, and they're part of a folk style that has been around a long time. Through their recordings, the Carter Family developed and popularized a unique style of playing. Maybelle Carter, the mother of June Carter Cash (wife of Johnny Cash), was a guitarist who played only in the keys of C and G. She would take the melody of a song and play it on the bass strings of the guitar, but would also strum the chords (using mostly the flick/back style) on the top strings to keep the rhythm. In the Carter Family recording of "John Hardy Was a Desperate Little Man," the voice can be heard in unison with the bass melody of the guitar. This provided a new and unique sound that became very popular. Many artists such as Duane Eddy, Woody Guthrie, Merle Travis, Bob Dylan, and Phil Ochs adapted this style to their own playing. It is strongly communicative, impressive to hear, and lots of fun to play.

Back Home Again

Words and Music by
John Denver

Many of John Denver's songs can be played in Carter Family style. Here's an excerpt from one of them.

From here, the tune will be transposed to C major—this allows for enough room in the bass to fit melody notes while playing chords or chord fragments on the treble strings. When you do your own arrangements, remember always to look at the range of a song's melody (highest and lowest notes) to determine if you will be able to play it in the bass.

Also note that it's not important to play every note of the original melody in the bass. You have to leave some room between the notes to strum the chords. Select the most important notes—the ones that define the melody—and stick to their basic rhythms. Note, too, that you can deviate slightly from a melody for the sake of a bass line. With all of that in mind, here is the "bare bones" tune in C.

Here's the final product: a Carter-style arrangement based on the bass–flick/back strum learned earlier in this chapter. Maybelle Carter used a thumb pick on the bass strings and brushed the chords with her fingers instead of a pick. You can also use your thumbnail or even a flatpick here.

TRACK 26

Flick/backs, bass runs, hammer-ons, pull-offs—when will it all end? The true answer is "never," but isn't that a good thing? You just have to listen to a few of John Denver's recordings to know that what you can do on the guitar is limited only by your imagination.

Now that you have the techniques of strumming under your fingertips—or have worn out 20 flatpicks working on this chapter—let's change course and explore the playing style known as fingerpicking.

Fingerpicking Techniques

■ A Very Basic Arpeggio

At this point, you might need a little refresher course in how to use the right-hand fingers properly. This pattern is the same as one encountered as an example in the beginning of the book, but now you should *really nail it*, as it's a major building block for other patterns. By the way, in case you didn't know, an *arpeggio* is literally a "broken chord"—the notes sound one at a time rather than together as in strumming. Every fingerpicking accompaniment pattern you use is, in some way, an arpeggio in disguise.

So, position the fingers and thumb as follows. Your thumb should rest on the 4th string (make sure it's a bit further to the left of the other fingers), and your ring, middle, and index fingers should be poised to pluck the 1st, 2nd, and 3rd strings, respectively. Rest your right arm on the edge of the guitar. It should touch the guitar near the bridge and with the part of the forearm closest to the elbow. Your forearm and shoulder should remain relaxed at all times.

Notice that the wrist is essentially straight. When you actually pluck the string, the nail or fingertip isn't really parallel to the string—it strikes the string at an angle.

Now, play the 4th string with your thumb using a downward motion. This is followed, one at a time, by the index, middle, and ring fingers hitting their assigned strings. When you feel comfortable with the 1st through 4th strings, try moving the pattern about to the other two sets of four strings (2nd through 5th and 3rd through 6th).

TRACK 27

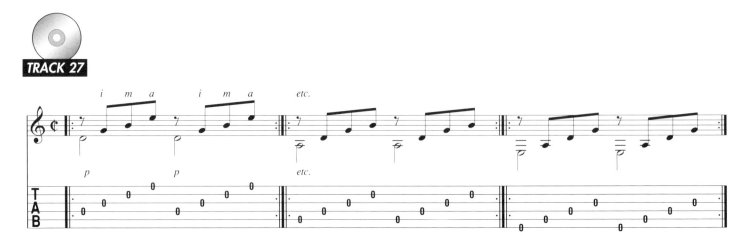

This simple arpeggio above is a useful fingerpicking pattern that you will use quite often in one way or another. But it isn't the only one by a long shot!

■ Outside-Inside Picking

This pattern can take a little getting used to—particularly the movement of the thumb—but it's well worth the effort, as other patterns are built on it.

This is a three-finger pattern; you should use only the thumb, index, and middle fingers. The gist of this is that you should play the "outside" notes (generally, those on the top and bottom strings of the chord) one after the other, followed by two "inside" notes (two somewhere on the strings between the "outside" notes). The basic order of the fingers here is thumb–middle–thumb–index. You may want to try just tapping your right-hand fingers on a table in that order, just to get a feel for which finger should move when.

Now, hold down a C chord and look at the music below. Play the outside strings of the chord (the notes on the 5th and then the 1st string), followed by those on the inside strings (the notes on the 3rd and then the 2nd string).

TRACK 28

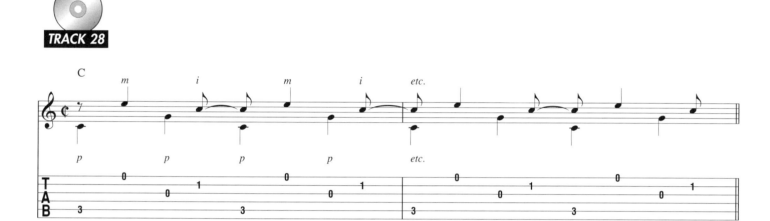

You can also play variations on the outside-inside pattern. Here's one with the treble pattern shifted to the 2nd, 3rd, and 4th strings.

TRACK 29

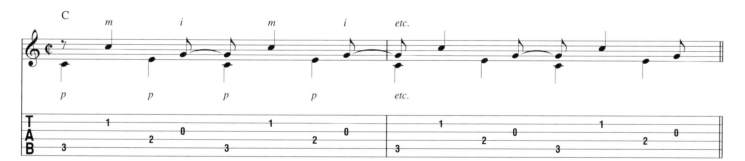

These two variants both come in handy. Note that the pattern has been changed to thumb–index–thumb–middle.

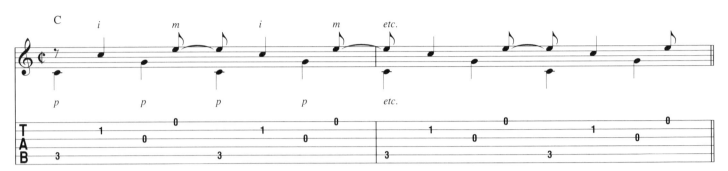

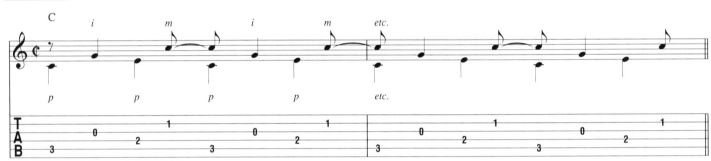

When you do this type of picking on your own, choose four strings to fingerpick for each chord based on either how they sound together or which notes you want to emphasize. The notes don't necessarily have to be on adjacent strings. It's a good idea to use the root of the chord as the bass (the first "thumb note"), but this is only a suggestion.

This Old Guitar

Words and Music by
John Denver

This song is one of my personal favorites (for obvious reasons). It's a gentle and touching tribute to the instrument that John Denver loved. Here are the lyrics, chords, and melody of the first Verse.

And here is that same Verse with John Denver's own choices for an outside-inside picking accompaniment. If you'd like to play along with Denver's recording of the song, capo up two frets.

■ Pinching

When you strum with a pick and want to hear more than one note at a time, you can strike notes only on *adjacent* strings. It's impossible to play a bass note and a note on the 1st string with the pick alone.

One of the great features of fingerpicking is that you can play several notes at one time, regardless of whether their strings are adjacent to each other. You can make the bass and treble parts move away from each other, towards each other, or in the same direction. The individual lines can function independently. This is the reason that fingerpicking, as many classical, fingerstyle jazz, blues, and ragtime guitarists have discovered, can mimic the sound of a keyboard instrument, such as the harpsichord or the piano. The thumb can function as a keyboardist's left hand with an independent bass part, while the fingers can pick an independent "right-hand" melody above that bass.

When you are fingerpicking a bass note with one or more treble notes, the thumb and fingers move towards each other. With your right hand, place your thumb on the 6th string and your middle finger on the 1st string. To play these notes together, you simultaneously pluck downwards with your thumb and upwards with your middle finger. The motion looks like a pinch. Try the following two exercises that include this technique. Practice them very slowly at first.

With this first one, when you feel comfortable with the *m–i–m–i* pattern, try *a–m–a–m*.

TRACK 33

And now with this second one, when you have the *i–m–i–m* pattern in your fingers, try *m–a–m–a*.

TRACK 34

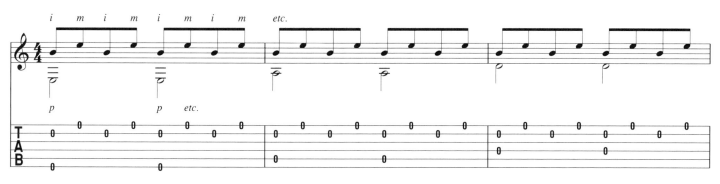

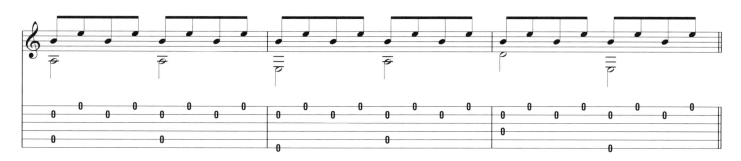

■ Calypso Picking

Calypso picking gets its name from its palm-swaying rhythm. It is mainly a matter of accents. In 4/4, for instance, a calypso rhythm divides a measure of eight eighth notes into 3+3+2 instead of the old familiar 2+2+2+2 or 4+4.

So, instead of this. . .

TRACK 35

. . .or this. . .

TRACK 36

. . .you have this.

Tap out the previous three examples on a tabletop. Repeat the third until you can feel its interesting arrangement of accents. There you have it!

Once you've mastered the pinch technique within the rhythm of the calypso pattern, you'll be fairly drooling for one of those drinks served in a coconut shell with an umbrella in it. Work on this right-hand exercise to familiarize your brain and fingers with playing in "calypso time." Repeat as necessary until it feels natural, and *don't forget the accents!*

Leaving on a Jet Plane

Words and Music by
John Denver

"Leaving on a Jet Plane" is in standard 4/4 time, but this arrangement injects it with a sort of calypso patois. This is one of John Denver's best-known songs, and it was a big hit for Peter, Paul and Mary. With all of the skills you have learned so far, this accompaniment pattern for "Jet Plane" should be quite easy to play. There are some jazzier chords in this arrangement than those used in the original song: Amaj7, Dmaj7, and Esus4. They are no more difficult to play, but their special sound and "ear feel" compliment the music and words quite well.

TRACK 39

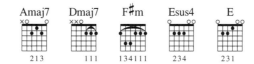

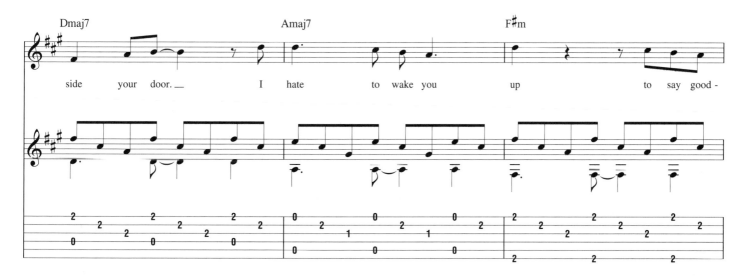

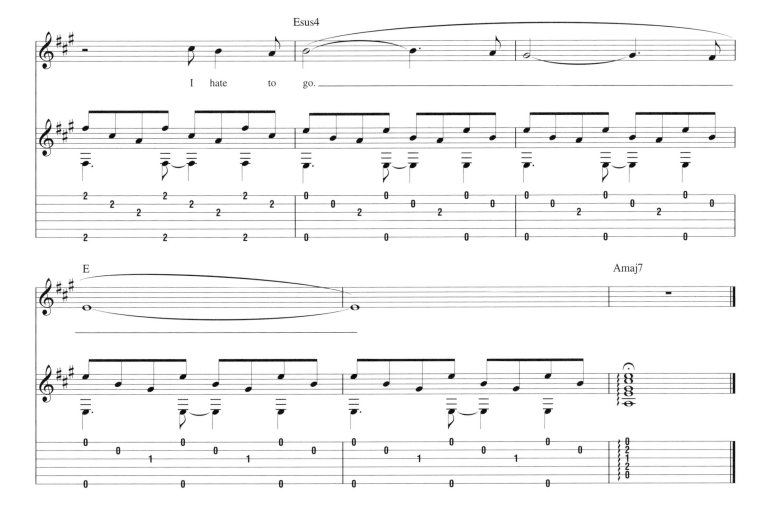

I hate to go. _____

Additional lyrics

2. There's so many times I've let you down,
   So many times I've played around,
   I tell you now they don't mean a thing.
   Every place I go I'll think of you,
   Every song I sing I'll sing for you,
   When I come back I'll bring your wedding ring.

   Chorus

3. Now the time has come to leave you,
   One more time let me kiss you,
   Then close your eyes, I'll be on my way,
   Dream about the days to come,
   When I won't have to leave alone,
   About the times I won't have to say:

   Chorus

Playing Two Treble Strings at Once

This is very easy to do. Don't fret anything with your left hand for now, but anchor your right thumb on the 6th string and your index finger on the 3rd. Plant your middle and ring fingers on the 2nd and 1st strings, respectively. Imagine that your middle and ring fingers are glued together so that they play the 1st and 2nd strings at once. It should look and feel like you are moving one big finger. Play the pattern *p–i–ma–i*, keeping your fingers moving in an even eighth note rhythm. Repeat as necessary until you feel comfortable.

TRACK 40

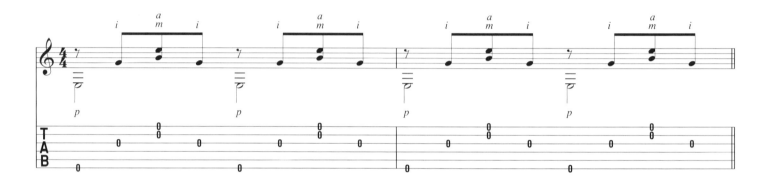

Fingerpicking in 3/4 Time

Let's adapt this two-strings-at-once pattern for songs that are in 3/4 time. All that you learned about playing 3/4 rhythms in *Strumming Techniques* applies here. Otherwise, all that you need to do is take away one beat per measure (here, the third quarter note beat) from the previous example in 4/4. Your thumb still plays on beat 1.

TRACK 41

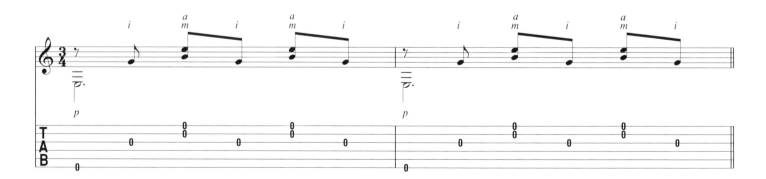

Annie's Song

Words and Music by
John Denver

Although John Denver wrote most of his songs in 4/4, he chose to write this, one of his biggest hits, in 3/4. It shows his ability to express his love through the natural world he knew so well: the forests, mountains, and streams of Colorado. When he sings "You fill up my senses like a night in a forest" you can tell he spent many nights there, sleeping under the stars.

This arrangement is similar to the one John himself used. You are free to use different basses, or even to play different treble strings; just remember to keep the pattern consistent. For a song like this, the guitar should provide a background accompaniment so the listener can be free to focus on the melody and lyric.

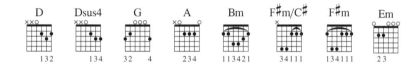

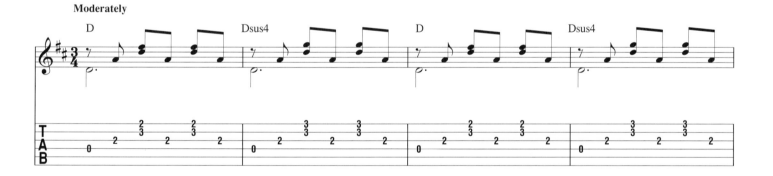

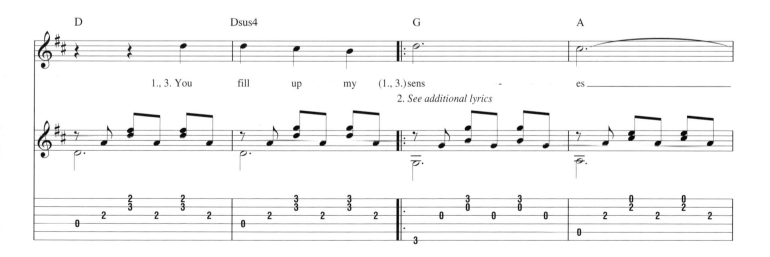

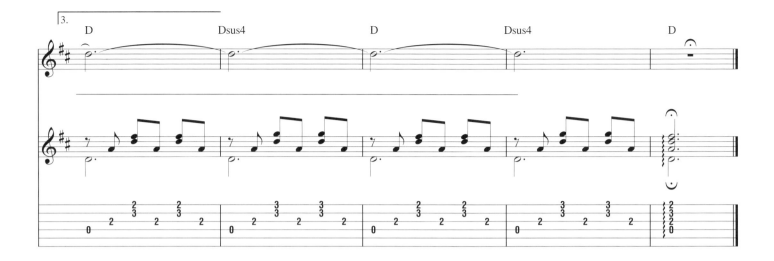

Additional lyrics

2. Come let me love you,
   Let me give my life to you,
   Let me drown in your laughter,
   Let me die in your arms,
   Let me lay down beside you,
   Let me always be with you.
   Come let me love you,
   Come love me again.

■ Basic Travis Picking

So, who is "Travis" anyway? Well, he was country guitarist, singer, and songwriter Merle Travis (1917–1983). He popularized a style of picking the guitar that he learned in his native Kentucky, based on the African-American banjo styles used in that part of the country. It features a steady quarter note bass line, played with the thumb, and syncopated melody notes that fill in the space between the bass notes. Another descriptive name for the style is *thumb picking*.

Travis realized that with this technique he could play melody and bass at the same time. It gave him the ability to add instrumental breaks to his songs, as well as perform full instrumental arrangements of the pop and jazz tunes of the day.

It is a relatively easy technique to learn, but because of the constant syncopation of the melody against the steady bass, it sounds much more difficult than it really is.

Books have been written about this picking pattern and its many uses in folk, country, jazz, and pop styles. I have devised a four-step method that quickly teaches you the basics, so just pick up your guitar and move to the Travis Pick Express Aisle where you can check out with the skills necessary to play this pattern in a hurry.

Step 1—Conquer the Bass

This is the easiest, and yet the most important step in the pattern. The bass, played in quarter notes with the thumb, alternates between the 6th (open) and 4th (2nd fret) strings in this example and provides the foundation for the melody notes that we will add later.

TRACK 43

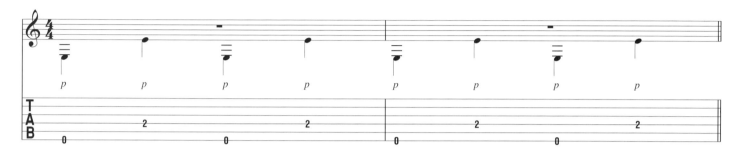

Don't rush off this step too quickly. It seems easy to play when you don't have anything else going on in the treble strings. Once you add in those extra notes with your fingers, the bass can become obscured rhythmically if it has not already been made solid by practice.

The rest of the four steps involve filling in the eighth note gaps between the bass notes (accompaniment), and then adding melody notes above the bass.

Step 2—Add Some Accompaniment

For the next step, one eighth note (3rd string, open G) is added on the upbeat of beat 2. It is played with the index finger.

TRACK 44

Step 3—Add a Pinch

Now, on beat 1, play the 1st string with your ring finger at the same time that you play the first bass note with your thumb. Unlike in calypso picking, the pinch is played only on the first beat of each measure. Repeat this enough times so that you feel comfortable with everything that's going on.

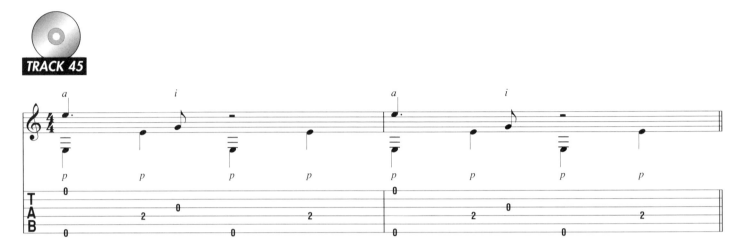

Step 4—Complete the Pattern

One more accompaniment note is added here. Play the 2nd string on the upbeat of beat 3 with your middle finger. You should now be hearing a steady bass line, above which is the syncopated melody on the treble strings. That's it!

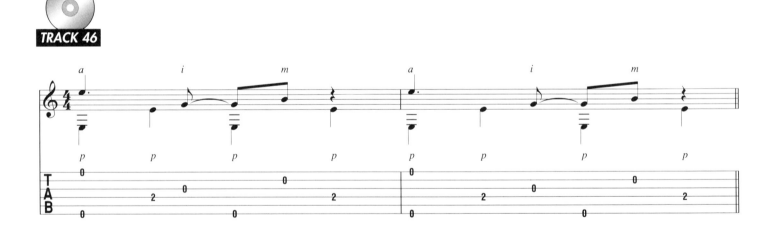

I Guess He'd Rather Be in Colorado

Words and Music by
Bill Danoff and Taffy Nivert Danoff

Travis picking can sound great as a repetitive picking pattern, as demonstrated by this next John Denver song—which always leaves me *pining* for the spruces! What makes Travis picking work so well in this song is the interplay between a very smooth-moving melody (one that also has very few melodic skips) and the syncopated sound of the right-hand pattern. When you vary the strings you are hitting and add in some hammer-ons and pull-offs, then your picking can really sound great! Since you've been picking for a while now, I didn't stop at a basic Travis pick arrangement— I took the liberty of adding in some embellishments that I would use to accompany the song.

TRACK 47

Easy Tempo

I guess he'd rath - er be in Col - o - ra - do, _____

2., 3. See additional lyrics

he'd rath - er spend his time out where the

sky looks like a pearl af - ter a rain. _____ Once a-

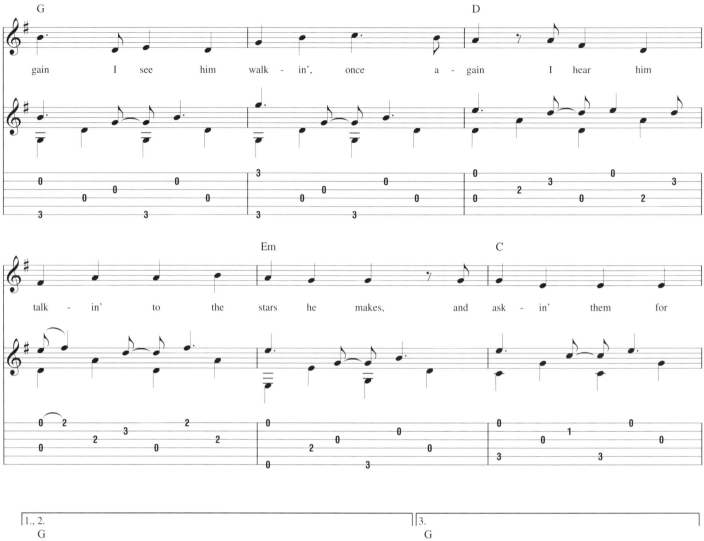

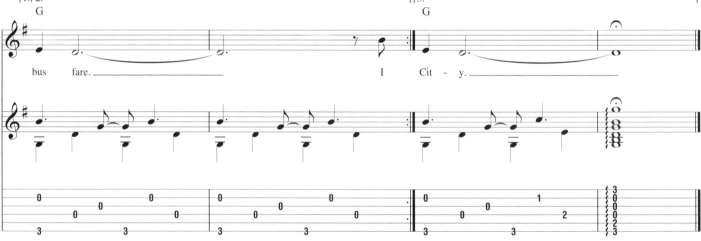

Additional lyrics

2. I guess he'd rather be in Colorado,
   He'd rather play his banjo in the morning when the moon is scarcely gone.
   In the dawn the subway's comin',
   In the dawn I hear him hummin'
   Some old song he wrote of love in Boulder Canyon.

3. I guess he'd rather be in Colorado,
   I guess he'd rather work out where the only thing you earn is what you spend.
   In the end, up in his office,
   In the end a quiet cough is all he has to show;
   He lives in New York City.

Technique Tip #5
Adding a Countermelody to a Travis Pick

In many basic arrangements, there are often "unused" notes in chords—notes on strings that aren't played in the pattern, yet have a left-hand finger holding them down. Also, in many chords there are usually one or two left-hand fingers that are just "hanging out" with nothing to do. So, why not put all of this to work? For example, the excerpt below is a simple picking pattern over a C chord, but there's an added line on top. It's just a simple scale fragment—a little countermelody—starting on C on the 2nd string and advancing step-wise to G on the 1st string.

Now, here's that same basic arrangement set in a Travis Pick feel. The syncopated rhythm of the melody seems to move independently of the steady bass. This is the effect you want here. Many chords and song situations lend themselves to inserting a scale or countermelody easily, but some are easier to add things to than others. Familiarity with chord forms and a little creativity can help you greatly in this department

■ Travis Picking with Pick and Fingers

Flatpickers, now it's your turn—you can play a version of the Travis pick that uses a combination of pick and fingers. Many fine acoustic folk/rock guitarists such as Richard Thompson and Paul Brady use this technique. While it limits the number of fingers you can use to pluck the strings (the index finger is now involved in holding the pick), it has an edgy sound that can be appealing. Here's what the right hand should look like.

The middle and ring fingers handle the melody, and you can usually play all of the melody notes with just one finger. The flatpick plays all of the bass notes.

Sweet Surrender

Words and Music by
John Denver

Here's an arrangement of the Chorus of "Sweet Surrender" that demonstrates the pick-and-fingers technique. Remember to play all of the bass notes with the pick. You can play the melody line with your middle finger, your ring finger, or a combination of both. For instance, you can use your middle finger for the notes on the 2nd string and your ring finger for the notes on the 1st string.

TRACK 50

For an extra effect, you can rest your palm on the bridge of the guitar. Let it touch only the bass strings so that when you play they have a muted sound. This creates a very effective color that is used in many fingerpicking styles.

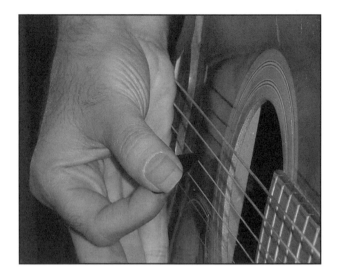

■ Arranging

Once you become adept at playing accompaniments using the Travis pick—meaning that you can play simple scales, control the bass notes, and incorporate techniques such as hammer-ons and pull-offs—you are ready to create your own homegrown arrangements.

To really grasp how to arrange a song takes both time and training. There are so many elements that go into making an arrangement: a good understanding of harmony and part writing, a broad knowledge of styles, creativity, a well-developed guitar technique, a good ear, etc. This book introduces only the basic concepts as far as these are concerned, but there is much you can do with even this much. The first step towards being skilled at arranging songs is to study other people's arrangements (such as those by John Denver!) and choose what you like or don't like about them. By borrowing from other players' styles, you can come up with one that works for you.

Before you begin to create an arrangement, it is best to have a plan and to make decisions about where you want to go with it. Here's a good game plan for when you're just starting out.

First, you should choose a song. Never dismiss the obvious! It is best to pick a song with a melody that falls within a limited range of notes. For one of your first arrangements, you don't want to be stuck figuring out what chord to use with a melody note that is five ledger lines above the staff. You might also want to choose a slow song with no key changes. Keep everything simple.

Next, you should choose a key for your arrangement. You may find that the original key of the song works well when you are just singing and strumming chords. However, if you are dealing with an instrumental arrangement where you must play both melody and harmony at the same time, you'll need the melody notes to fall within the fingerings of the chords. Also, watch that the bass and melody notes played simultaneously don't exceed the stretch of your left-hand fingers! The traditional guitar keys—C major, F major, and keys with sharps in their signatures—work best. They allow us as guitarists to take advantage of playing open strings as well as bass notes that don't require fretting.

Next, you should choose a picking style or pattern that will work for *most* of the song. Be aware that you may have to break away from the pattern at times due to rhythm and meter changes. You can base your arrangement on either a regular, free-flowing pattern such as the outside-inside style, or something a little more rigid like Travis picking with a quarter note bass line anchoring the harmony and tempo. Often, the picking pattern can be determined by the time signature and tempo of the song, but if you have mastered all of the patterns in this chapter, you may often find that there isn't always *just one* pattern that will work. Much of the time, the best choice is to keep the pattern changing throughout the song or to combine patterns and vary their use. In the end, the arrangement may no longer sound like a pattern at all, but rather a filigree of notes that decorates the melody and adds dimension to the harmony.

When you create a fingerpicking arrangement as a vocal accompaniment, it is expected that the pattern will sound repetitive and regular in order to keep the focus on the sung melody and lyrics. If you are creating a solo guitar arrangement, then a regular pattern may not be the best choice. There may be spots where you will want to call more attention to the melody or another element and may wish to break the pattern. These sections will stand out and sound improvised or composed, depending upon your abilities as a player and arranger.

Now it's time to consider the melody, the most important element here. When creating an arrangement, one often has the flexibility to change the rhythm of the melody by using syncopation or other rhythmic devices in order to fit it with the picking pattern. If you start with a simple tune, this won't be much of a problem. After a while, you should be able to hear when it is best to throw in a little syncopation.

The harmony is the last major element to be dealt with. Although you should try to stick close to the songwriter's original ideas, oftentimes you can substitute similar chords to add variety and interest. For instance, if a song calls for a C major chord (C–E–G), an A minor chord (A–C–E) or E minor chord (E–G–B) could perhaps be used instead, depending on the melody and the overall feel off the song. Never be afraid to experiment!

As an addendum, don't be afraid to infuse your arrangement with a few "extras" such as bass runs, hammer-ons, and pull offs. Generally, good opportunities for any or all of these will present themselves once you've created the basic arrangement and have played it through a few times.

Poems, Prayers and Promises

Words and Music by
John Denver

This solo guitar arrangement—which includes elements of Denver's own—is based on the Travis pick, but in key spots I chose a more standard chord melody arrangement in a folk/classical style. It gets across the essence of the melody and highlights the changes between the sections of the song.

Note that this arrangement utilizes what is called *drop D tuning*—the low E string is tuned down a whole step to D. This low note can really come in handy for songs in the keys of D or G. Because of this tuning, however, note that some of the assumed fingerings must change, since all of the bass notes on the E string have been altered by a whole step (two frets).

While you're at it, try to identify some of the elements of folk guitar playing used here—hammer-ons, pull-offs, bass runs, etc. Isolate the sections that are tricky for you and work on them separately as technique exercises.

TRACK 51

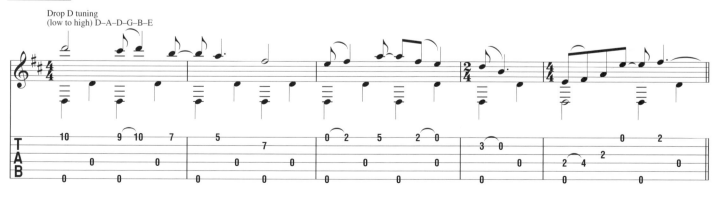

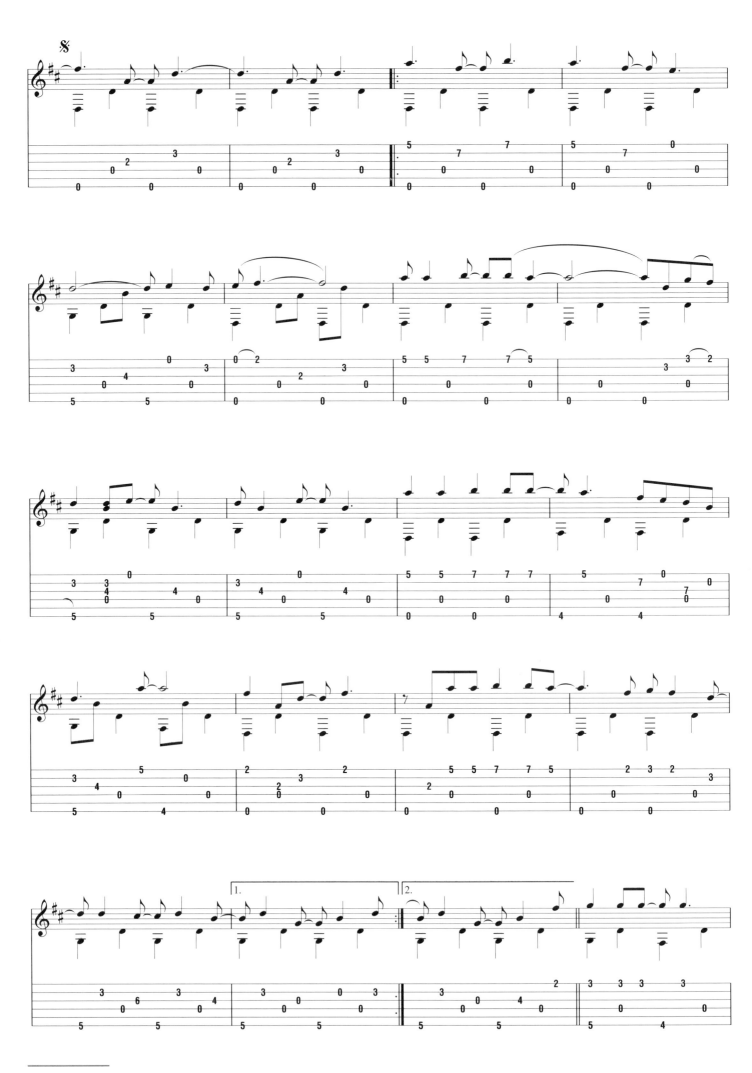

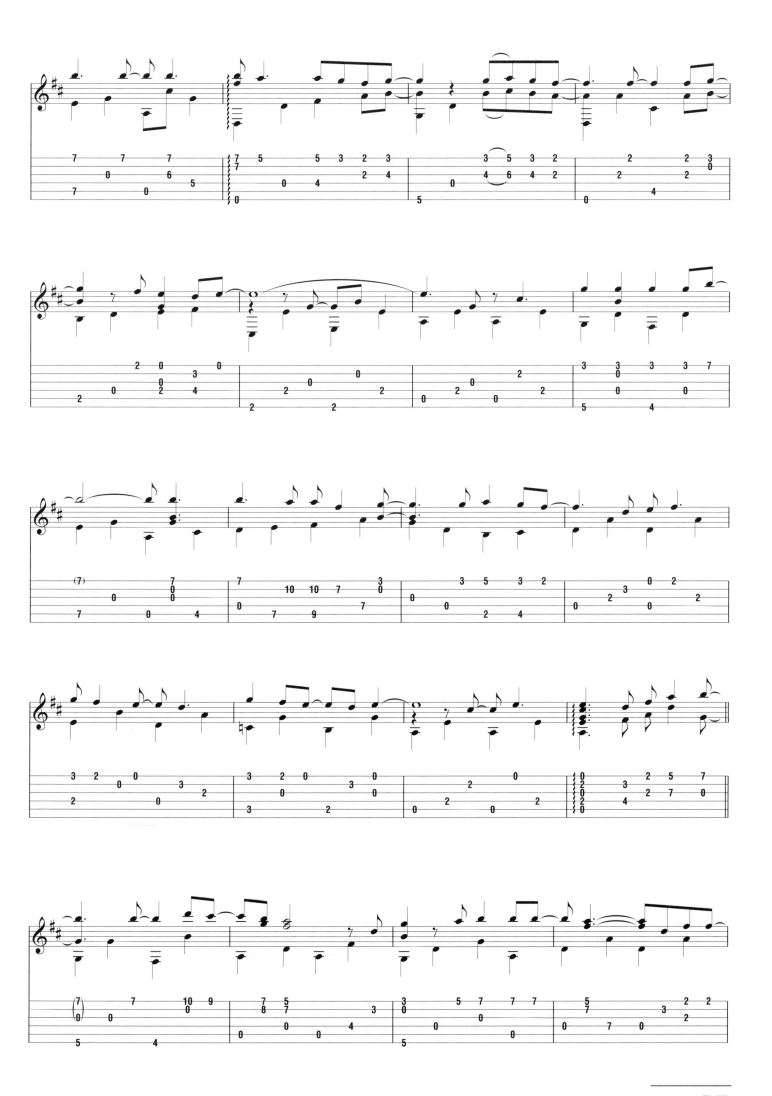

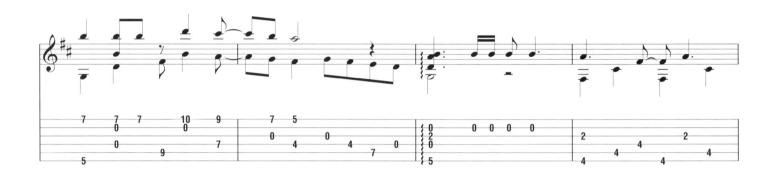

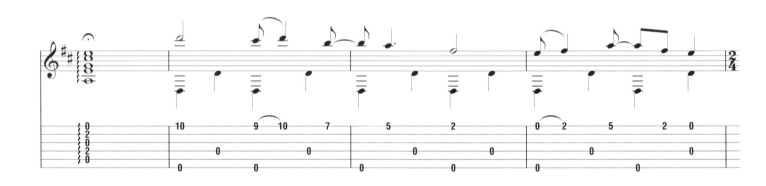

To Coda ⊕

D.S. al Coda
(take 2nd ending)

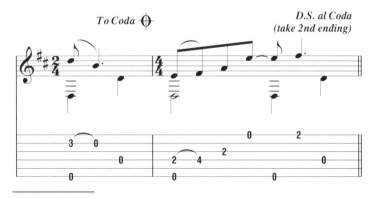

⊕ *Coda*

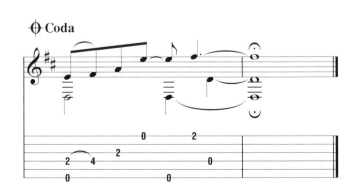

Epilogue

There have been few guitarists who did as much for popularizing folk music as John Denver. His political beliefs were just as strong as those of the folk singers who preceded him, but he chose for his own part to approach folk music as not just a vehicle of protest, but as a more universal language of songs about love, nature, and portraits of places. In a sense, he returned folk music to its roots.

By playing his songs and learning his guitar style, you've touched upon the great wealth that folk music has to offer. As a guitarist, no matter how long you have been playing, there will always be so much more for you to explore. John Denver's music can inspire one to go even further than one imagined. Given the right conditions, he would have taken his guitar into space and wrote about what he saw there. Is anyone else ready to accept that mission?

Goodbye Again

Words and Music by
John Denver

There is no more fitting way to end this method book than with John Denver's "Goodbye Again." My arrangement here is free, not adhering to any one fingerpicking pattern, but rather using the melody and lyrics as guides.

TRACK 52

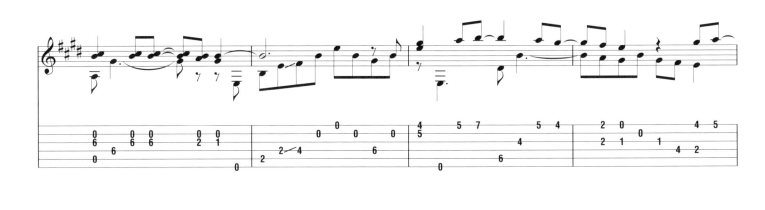

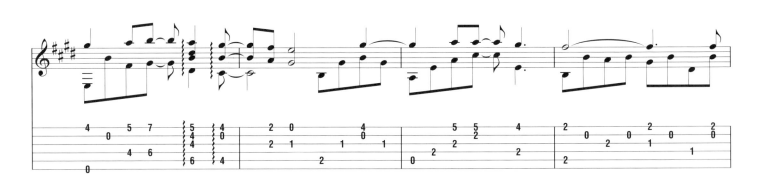

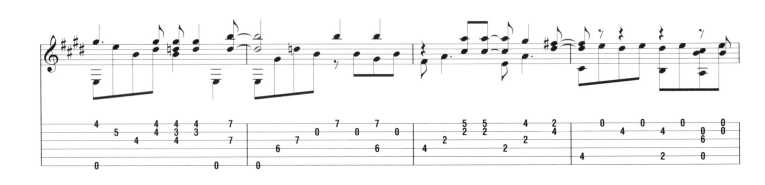

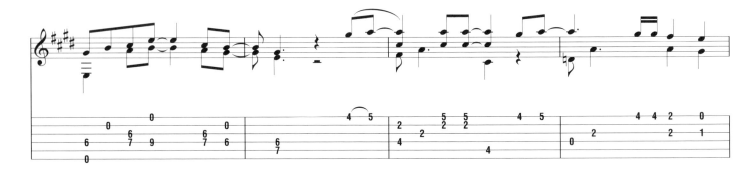

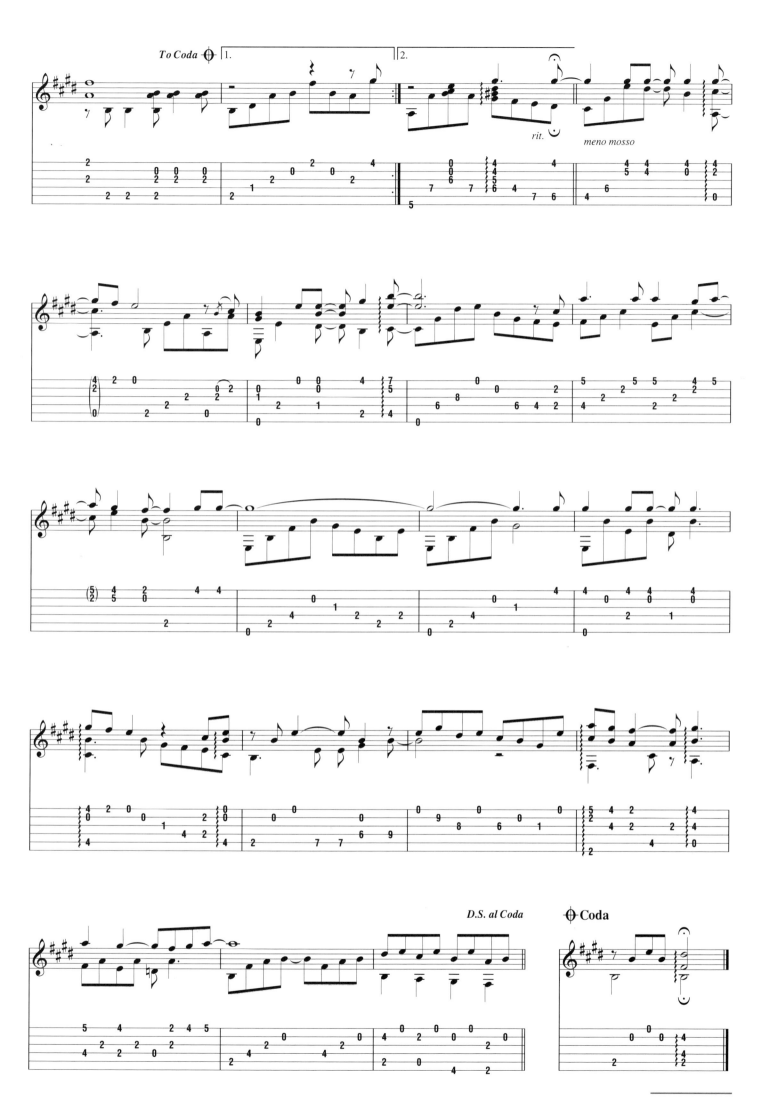

Cherry Lane Music is your source for
JOHN DENVER SONGBOOKS!

PIANO/VOCAL BOOKS

JOHN DENVER ANTHOLOGY
A collection of 54 of this music legend's greatest tunes, including: Annie's Song • Follow Me • Leaving on a Jet Plane • Rocky Mountain High • Sunshine on My Shoulders • and more, plus a biography and John's reflections on his many memorable songs.
_____02502165 Piano/Vocal/Guitar $22.95

THE BEST OF JOHN DENVER – EASY PIANO
A collection of 18 Denver classics arranged for easy piano. Contains: Leaving on a Jet Plane • Take Me Home, Country Roads • Rocky Mountain High • Follow Me • and more.
_____02505512 Easy Piano $9.95

THE BEST OF JOHN DENVER – PIANO SOLOS
Best of John Denver – Piano Solos is a fabulous collection of 10 greatest hits from the legendary country artist. It includes many of his major hits including: Annie's Song • Leaving on a Jet Plane • Rocky Mountain High • and Take Me Home, Country Roads.
_____02503629 Piano Solo $10.95

JOHN DENVER – A CELEBRATION OF LIFE
The matching folio to the legendary songwriter/performer's album features some of his most popular songs. Includes: Rocky Mountain High • Leaving on a Jet Plane • Whispering Jesse • and more, plus photos and biographical information.
_____02502227 Piano/Vocal/Guitar...............................$14.95

A JOHN DENVER CHRISTMAS
A delightful collection of Christmas songs and carols recorded by John Denver. Includes traditional carols (Deck the Halls • Hark! The Herald Angels Sing • The Twelve Days of Christmas) as well as such contemporary songs as: A Baby Just Like You • Christmas for Cowboys • Christmas Like a Lullaby • and The Peace Carol.
_____02500002 Piano/Vocal/Guitar...............................$14.95

JOHN DENVER: THE COMPLETE LYRICS
An extremely gifted singer/songwriter, John Denver possessed the unique ability to marry melodic music with gentle, thought-provoking words that endeared him to his countless fans. Now, for the first time ever, John Denver's lyrics have been printed in their entirety: no other book like this exists! It contains lyrics to more than 200 songs, and includes an annotated discography showing all the songs, and an index of first lines. This collection also features an introduction by Tom Paxton, and a foreword from Milt Okun, John Denver's first record producer, and the founder of Cherry Lane Music.
_____02500459 ....$16.95

JOHN DENVER'S GREATEST HITS
This collection combines all of the songs from Denver's three best-selling greatest hits albums. 34 songs in all, including: Leaving on a Jet Plane • For Baby (For Bobbie) • Thank God I'm a Country Boy • Annie's Song • Perhaps Love • I Want to Live.
_____02502166 Piano/Vocal/Guitar $17.95

JOHN DENVER – A LEGACY OF SONG
This collection celebrates one of the world's most popular and prolific entertainers. Features 25 of John's best-loved songs with his commentary on each: Annie's Song • Fly Away • Leaving on a Jet Plane • Rocky Mountain High • Sunshine on My Shoulders • Take Me Home, Country Roads • Thank God I'm a Country Boy • and more, plus a biography, discography, reflections on John's numerous accomplishments, and photos spanning his entire career.
_____02502151 Piano/Vocal/Guitar Softcover $24.95
_____02502152 Piano/Vocal/Guitar Hardcover $34.95

JOHN DENVER & THE MUPPETS – A CHRISTMAS TOGETHER
Back by popular demand! This book featuring John Denver, Kermit, and all the Muppets includes 12 holiday songs: A Baby Just like You • Carol for a Christmas Tree • Christmas Is Coming • The Christmas Wish • Deck the Halls • Have Yourself a Merry Little Christmas • Little Saint Nick • Noel: Christmas Eve, 1913 • The Peace Carol • Silent Night, Holy Night • The Twelve Days of Christmas • We Wish You a Merry Christmas.
_____02500501 Piano/Vocal/Guitar...............................$9.95

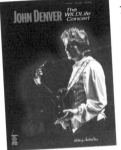

JOHN DENVER – THE WILDLIFE CONCERT
This matching folio to John Denver's second live album – a two-CD set accompanying a cable TV special and home video – features 29 fabulous tracks: Amazon • Annie's Song • Bet on the Blues • Calypso • Darcy Farrow • Eagles and Horses • Falling Out of Love • The Harder They Fall • Is It Love? • Leaving on a Jet Plane • Me and My Uncle • A Song for All Lovers • Sunshine on My Shoulders • You Say That the Battle Is Over • and more.
_____02500326 Piano/Vocal/Guitar...............................$17.95

P/V/G SHEET MUSIC

_____02504223 **Annie's Song**...$3.95
_____02504206 **Follow Me**..$3.95
_____02504181 **For You** $3.95
_____02504225 **Leaving on a Jet Plane** $3.95
_____02509538 **Perhaps Love** $3.95
_____02504219 **Sunshine on My Shoulders**................................$3.95
_____02504214 **Take Me Home, Country Roads** $3.95
_____02509523 **Thank God I'm a Country Boy**............................$3.95

GUITAR BOOKS

JOHN DENVER ANTHOLOGY FOR EASY GUITAR
This superb collection of 42 great Denver songs made easy for guitar includes: Annie's Song • Leaving on a Jet Plane • Take Me Home, Country Roads • plus performance notes, a biography, and Denver's thoughts on the songs.
_____02506878 Easy Guitar.......................................$15.95

JOHN DENVER AUTHENTIC GUITAR STYLE
12 never-before-published acoustic guitar note-for-note transcriptions of the most popular songs by John Denver. Includes the hits: Annie's Song • Sunshine on My Shoulders • Take Me Home, Country Roads • and more.
_____02506901 Acoustic Guitar Transcriptions.......................$14.95

THE BEST OF JOHN DENVER
Over 20 of Denver's best-known hits spanning his 25-year career! Includes: Annie's Song • Leaving on a Jet Plane • Rocky Mountain High • Thank God I'm a Country Boy • Sunshine on My Shoulders • and more.
_____02506879 Easy Guitar $9.95

JOHN DENVER – GREATEST HITS FOR FINGERSTYLE GUITAR
For the first time ever, 11 favorite Denver standards in fingerstyle arrangements that incorporate the melodies of the songs and can therefore be played as solo guitar pieces or vocal accompaniments. Includes: Annie's Song • Leaving on a Jet Plane • Rocky Mountain High • and more.
_____02506928 Fingerstyle Guitar.................................$14.95

For a complete listing of available Cherry Lane titles, please visit our web site at **www.cherrylane.com**

CHERRY LANE MUSIC COMPANY
6 East 32nd Street, New York, NY 10016
Quality in Printed Music

EXCLUSIVELY DISTRIBUTED BY
HAL•LEONARD® CORPORATION
7777 W. BLUEMOUND RD. P.O. BOX 13819 MILWAUKEE, WI 53213